Balboa Press books may be ordered through booksellers or by contacting:

Balboa Press
A Division of Hay House
1663 Liberty Drive
Bloomington, IN 47403
www.balboapress.com
844-682-1282

ISBN: 978-1-9822-6727-8 (sc)
ISBN: 978-1-9822-6728-5 (e)

Library of Congress Control Number: 2021907601

Print information available on the last page.

Balboa Press rev. date: 04/13/2021

BALBOA.PRESS

Nicole Marie Castillo A.A.S

My Spiritual Awakening -
Up close & Personal

Ignite your intentions, heighten your intuition.

Table of Contents

Nourish Your Soul

Ingnite your intentions

Dedication

As I sit here today and reflect on my journey. I cannot help but think about my parents. May they rest in peace. I have overcome so much, and I only want to make them proud. I thank my mother for showing me how to be a strong single mother and to always show appreciation. I thank my father for telling me to never depend on anyone in life but yourself; To always stand up for yourself. If I could only go back to these specific moments in life. I would hug you both so tight and never let go. I just want to say thank you both for life and your wonderful words of wisdom. I dedicate this book to my parents. Without them both I am nobody. They built me from the inside out. Now, today I am an independent considerate woman.

Love and miss you both every day of my life.

· Madre Mia ·

I. *Letter to Past self*

Greetings Nicole,

You need a truthful reality check woman! I just want to acknowledge truth/facts regarding the serious issues you have encountered in your past. Do you remember how lonely you felt after you had to bury all your loved ones? You were alone and everybody you had left in your life.

The Universe and your spirit loved ones had your back, they never left your side. They nudged you into safety like you would not believe Nicole! You never cried alone; they were there- lifting you up. That is how you made it so far on your journey- still standing.

Do you remember how you felt overwhelmed with negativity in every direction you turned? You felt that because it was truly happening in every direction you turned. Do you remember how you always felt uncomfortable and unsafe when you left your house? People from all directions were plotting against you for years. They intentionally made your life hell & watched you drown in it.

Do you remember how you felt like you could not trust anybody in your life (including strangers)? You were right! There were so many people watching you, plotting against you- to take you down (literally physically down).

Do you remember that awful gut feeling you had in your own house? Your gut instinct was right! Even your own roommate was plotting against you. Yes! From your own house, sat on your sofa and watched you crumble- with a smile.

Do you remember how you always had that instinct feeling of having to be in defense mode? It is because they wanted to hurt you and Ysidro. Do you remember how you would question in your head, why do people look at me with so much hatred? People were attacking your reputation, making you out to be a heartless monster- for years.

Do you remember how you felt that people were whispering and spying on you behind your back? They were- lots of people. Do remember how you suspected people were following you? You were right! These people were even given specific details about when and where you were out and about; and/or followed you from your house.

Do you remember how you felt so overwhelmed with life within your heart and soul? People drove you to a point of temporary insanity; Kept at it for years. It was too much mental strain; more than one person could ever take on in a lifetime.

Do you remember when you told your best friend that you were under a psychic attack? You were! You had so much negative energy projected towards you for years- it resulted in a full-blown psychic attack.

I know you physically, mentally, and emotionally felt it and voiced it at times. Nobody believed you, they did not believe your words. They did not believe things could be so bad for you. You held it together well on the outside.

Do you remember how you felt that all your family, friends and co-workers looked at you with pure hate? That is because they were, you were right- again. They were all being mentally fed & accepted words of pure hatred towards you. That projected even more negative energy towards you.

Do you remember when you realized you were receiving messages from your spirit loved ones? That was when you started to conduct your research on spirituality. Your vibration elevated to a higher frequency. All the trauma you endured heightened your intuitive senses- Clairs, telepathy etc.

I feel your spirit loved ones-your angels have been guiding you all along. Your vibration was too low, you were not opened to acknowledge or receive. After all your trauma and PTSD, your intuition heightened.

Do you remember how you felt you had no privacy, how you could not even feel comfortable in your own home? That is because you do not have privacy in your own home, and people all around the world are watching your every move- Yes even in the restroom.

Do you remember when you quit your job, your vehicle got repossessed and you were being randomly awakened at night? That was the beginning of your intense spiritual awakening. That is why you were getting random thoughts of the past. All the actions that brought you mental and emotional abuse needed to be acknowledged as facts.

Do you remember how you felt so vulnerable in your heart and soul and questioned if people were plotting against you when you stepped outside your home? Everybody all around you is trying to set you up to get you arrested. Your intuition is right.

Do you remember you felt surrounded by negativity and suddenly people were coming to your house with supposedly "good intentions"? Every single person was trying to set you up, to get you arrested. That was around the time when you were praying with all your heart and soul, found faith & guidance within the bible- day after day.

I feel you were granted a reincarnation. It was an intense feeling, I know. You prayed, and you were saved by the creator. I feel that maybe you were rewarded for your battles you conquered in your past, the unnecessary mental & emotional trauma you endured.

Do you remember how you felt like you were under investigation by the FBI/CIA and your house was bugged? You were right! You have not had privacy for almost 5 years now. You have handled the situation quite well.

Do you remember when you had to set intense boundaries between yourself and all your family, friends, everybody you knew because of the negativity you were receiving? Good job! You made the best decision of your life, that was to follow your intuition.

Do you remember when you had a strong feeling of uplift like there was some sort of positive progress made in your life's favor? You felt that positive uplift because there was finally a break thru in your case. YES! you are under investigation, for child abuse.

There is no warrant for your arrest, so they cannot come and arrest you. A thorough investigation was finally conducted. The FBI/CIA finally followed thru in evidence leads they had access to at the start of this investigation.

I feel you have come a long way. You have discovered you are an awakened psychic empath, medium, solitary witch, and tarot reader. You are a soul of all nations, wanting to share your awakening and reincarnation with the world.

Share your journey, implement, and practice soul nourishment. Your soul is in alignment with its purpose. The world knows of your story and will gain knowledge of the existence of intuition. You have made a break thru in history.

Your spiritual awakening is one of a kind. I honestly believe nobody else in the world has ever encountered such an intense journey of life. Share your up-close personal feelings, thoughts, and actions taken in your spiritual awakening.

We are all souls, given a human body to carry on in our journey. Our soul is given lessons to learn and evolve. This book will give insight. Broken down into stages into your personal experience of your spiritual awakening. Other souls can utilize, gain knowledge, and implement on their journey.

Sincerely,
Me

II. *Introduction*

Greetings fellow spiritual souls,

I am a spiritual lightworker placed here on Earth in this lifetime. I have experienced a proven intense spiritual awakening. This spiritual awakening lasted years and years. As of today, I sit here a survivor of PTSD, Escaped death more than once. Lost my mental sanity a couple times. Lost a baby boy of 4 months pregnant, at 16 years old. Mourned the loss of both my parents and a husband. Was diagnosed with an autoimmune disorder. That is incurable. Went through some intense traumatic amount of adult bullying. All in a span of about 15 years. When I say I lost my mental sanity, I totally mean I lost my mind. I was hanging on to life by a thread. Attached myself to the wrong people for help. That also contributed to losing my mental sanity. Let's just say it made things worse in so many ways. I was kicked while I was down by many. During this time, I managed to maintain a fulltime job and parent my son. I did my best to put on a smile and face the world day after day. In 2016 things finally crumbled down for me. For the first time in my life, I lost my job. When I say I lost my job -I literally mean I got fired.

I started having unbearable headaches.

At this point things went down in a fast spiral for me. Out of instinct I started to reach out to God. (A higher power also known as and referred to in this treatise as God, Creator, Universe. This is my highest power in my life. It is a free country, and everyone has the right to their opinion) You can choose yours. All my life I have been very curious about intuition and its ability. After losing so many people in my lifetime around my late 20s. I would always wonder and question if spirits existed. All these questions I pondered upon. As I began to reach out to my higher power. I was literally directed to the bible, spirituality, and intuition. I took all the signs that the Universe gave me. I began to study spirituality, intuition, and its existence. In this treatise I will go into details of how I stumbled upon my intuition. I go into detail about intuition and different spirituality aspects. I also try my best to point out aspects that worked for me to build my spiritual practice and raise my vibration. I came across so much information. I would love to share it with the world. That is my purpose for this book. To speak to the world. To point out all the details that stood out to me during my spiritual awakening. I am not saying I have all the answers. I am saying I learned and experienced so much in a small period. As of today, I do not question if intuition exists. I know it exists.

I discovered I am a very highly intuitive soul. I even saw a spirit outside of my own house. It was my late husband Roberto. We never married. I did consider him a husband at one time in my life. He is also the father of my son. I was washing dishes and felt an urge to look outside the door. I did so and there he was. Roberto's spirit sitting on a chair that was sitting in my side porch. I got nervous and slammed the door shut. The feeling I got was he wanted to let me know I was not alone. At the time I was alone in the house. There were also issues going on with my son. That was out of my hands. I feel he just wanted to tell me he was still with me during my time of distress. At that time, it was confirmed to me spirits are real. I see it with my own eyes. Or maybe I should say I saw it with my third eye. Maybe not everyone could have witnessed him. I certainly did. I was extremely excited I had that capability. So, at this point I know intuition and spirit are real and it does exist on earth. After everything I have been through. I feel I have utilized intuition as a 6th sense. Without even knowing I was utilizing my intuition- I did. This book will lay out information I came across that I feel other souls could benefit from. I also point out my intuition abilities I came across. I am not trying to get rich off this book.

The most important thing to me is that people benefit from it. I just want to get my story across. I discovered I am telepathic. These things are real, they helped me out in the worst times of my life. My actual life was on the line. Discovering I was a highly intuitive individual was the best thing that ever happened to me in my life. It could help other people as well. Continue to read and let me know what you thought about the entire book. I am always open to questions and good feedback. Thank you for your time and support. I also want to point out I drew all the sketches in this book. I drew it as it came to me in my dreams, intuition or in my 3rd eye (clairvoyance). I personally believe they are connected to my past lives.

I discovered my artistic talent in my spiritual awakening. I never knew I could draw the way I do. I now consider myself an artist. I paint, draw, and use pastels in my artwork. It is quite soothing and helps with anxiety.

III. *Intuition Abilities*

Do you believe you have intuition abilities? The truth is every one of us does. Intuition has various forms of definition such as: Intuition: 1) a: the power or faculty of attaining to direct knowledge or cognition without evident rational thought and interference. b: immediate apprehension. c: knowledge or conviction gained by intuition. 2) quick and ready insight. (Merriam-Webster 1828) We as human beings all have insight intuition (also known as psychic abilities). It has been scientifically proven every individual has it. It can benefit our lives in all areas: personal, professional and in crisis situations.

According to Psychology today intuition is nonconscious thinking, more like the brain's autopilot. Scientist have repeatedly explained how information can trigger the brain without conscious awareness and positively effect decision- making (Psychology Today, n.d.). Intuition is processed automatically; known as the "highway hypnosis" This process occurs when a driver drives for miles without conscious thought about driving a car. Another example maybe a person walking down the street, may get lost in thought and find themselves at their destination. Without knowing how they got there (Psychology Today, n.d.).

There have been numerous of studies to determine intuition and our abilities. It has also been proven that our human heart and brain is in connection with how we receive intuition. In 2004 there was a proven science study to prove this fact. The proven study was conducted with presenting 30 calm and 15 emotionally arousing pictures to 26 participants: under two experimental conditions. Normal psycho-physiologic function was used as a baseline condition and a condition of physiological coherence. (R. McCarty, M. Atkinson, R. T. Bradley 2004). Base line measures included: skin conductance; the electroencephalogram (EEG), heartbeat -evoked components were received; and the electrocardiogram (ECG), which received cardiac decelerations/accelerations.

The results were used to measure where and when the brain and body intuitive information is processed (R. McCarty, M. Atkinson, R. T. Bradley 2004). The study's results resulted in two parts. The primary finding being, the heart's role in intuitive views presented here are: (1) the heart receives and responds to intuitive information; (2) a greater heart rate presented prior to future emotional stimuli verses calm stimuli; (3) significant gender differences in the processing of pre-stimulus information.

Part two reflects results indicating the brain's intuitive process; processed and data reflecting that pre-stimulus information from the heart is presented to the brain. It also reflected evidence that female participants were more attuned to intuitive information from the heart (R. McCarty, M. Atkinson, R. T. Bradley 2004).

The facts of realization of truth within intuition and spirituality have become so much more common in everyday life; Board certified medical doctors are incorporating this type of treatment into their medical practices. Judith Orloff M.D. is a board-certified psychiatrist and intuitive. According to article The Energy Psychiatry of Judith Orloff M.D, 2005. Dr Orloff has a private practice and incorporates energy, protocols of intuition and spirituality into her practice. She introduced the theory of energy psychiatry. "Energy psychiatry is a combination of conventional medicine, intuition, spirituality, and energy".

This is a new and important approach to conventional psychiatry. It is significant because it addresses problems and situations of which conventional medicine is unaware (Mason, R M.S, 2005) Dr Orloff indicates she coined the term "energy psychiatry" to explain a new form of psychotherapy. It reflects subtle energetic forms of health and behavior. It is considered energy medicine, that views our spirits and bodies as they manifest into subtle energies (Mason, R M.S, 2005).

Per Dr Orloff a patient will benefit tremendously while being treated with the integration of intuition, energy, and spirituality; The patient becomes attuned to subtle energies. This process grows with practice and an "inner guidance" system builds and gets stronger with daily use (Mason, R M.S, 2005) Per Dr Orloff "As a responsible physician, I feel that healthcare practitioners absolutely must incorporate intuition, spirituality and energy into patient care. Without this incorporation, patients are not being fully addressed" (Mason, R M.S, 2005)

Overall, it has been proven that intuition is a part of every human beings' role in the universe. We all receive intuition on different levels, depending on our sex; female or male. Utilizing our intuition can be considered an additional human being sense; in addition to our normal five senses. A person can make daily decisions based off intuition; It could be considered in our best interest. Our best interest for the higher good of our life journey.

References

Psychology Today (n.d.) Intuition. Retrieved from the website:

www.psychologytoday.com/us/basics/intuition

Mason, R M.S, (2005) The Energy Psychiatry of Judith Orloff M.D. Alternative & Complementary Therapies retrieved from https://www.liebertpub.com/doi/pdf/10.1089/act.2005.11.32

Mc Cartneym, R., Atkinson, M. and Bradley, R.T (2004). Electrophysiological Evidence of

Intuition. Part 1: The Surprising Role of the Heart. The Journal of Alternative and

Complementary Medicine. Volume 10, No. 1. Retrieved from: Electrophysiological Evidence of Intuition: Part 1. The Surprising Role of the Heart | HeartMath Institute

IV. *Self-Realization*

A) A process of questioning will begin. The existence of intuition, spirituality, and our human capabilities will begin to ponder within yourself. A question if God/ Universe/ Creator really exists. In the aspect of contributing positive guidance on your journey.

B) You may recognize a near-death experience in your past, traumatic life event and/or death of a loved one. These events would have been so traumatic to your soul. It would have impacted your ability to focus and disrupt your healthy state of mind.

C) For some people, even a nudge of curiosity may also just simply open your horizon. An opening from within your soul. A sense of awareness into the spirituality realm.

WCastillo
12/17

V. Searching & Seeking

A) Feeling a sudden urge/a calling from within your soul to learn more about spirituality and its existence. You will feel as if no information is satisfying for you and your soul.

B) Reaching out to spiritual teachers for answers and guidance. They all stepped forward and acted upon their soul calling, received from the universe.

C) Reading books, blogs, intuitive websites, and listening to informational audios. Utilize the tools that have been presented to the public. That is universe's way of informatively speaking out to the world.

D) Follow your gut instinct (solar plexus). It speaks to you from within your soul. Timing is guidance based on your specific journey. The universe will line you up with your timing of awakening.

VI. *Identifying synchronicity & signs*

A) The universe will start to align you with your journey's path. You will come across certain journey markers. Those markers will help open your awareness to direct you on your soul's journey.
B) You will start to recognize the same reoccurring synchronicities. Synchronicity can be reoccurring number patterns, reoccurring contact with souls, or maybe even a sense of direction to a particular place/community.
C) Approach the possibilities logically, weigh out any possibilities of being directed toward negative situations-use common sense as well.

=Twinflame=

=Synchronicity=

The experience of two or more events that are apparently casually unrelated or unlikley to occur together by chance yet are experienced as occuring together in a meaningful manner.

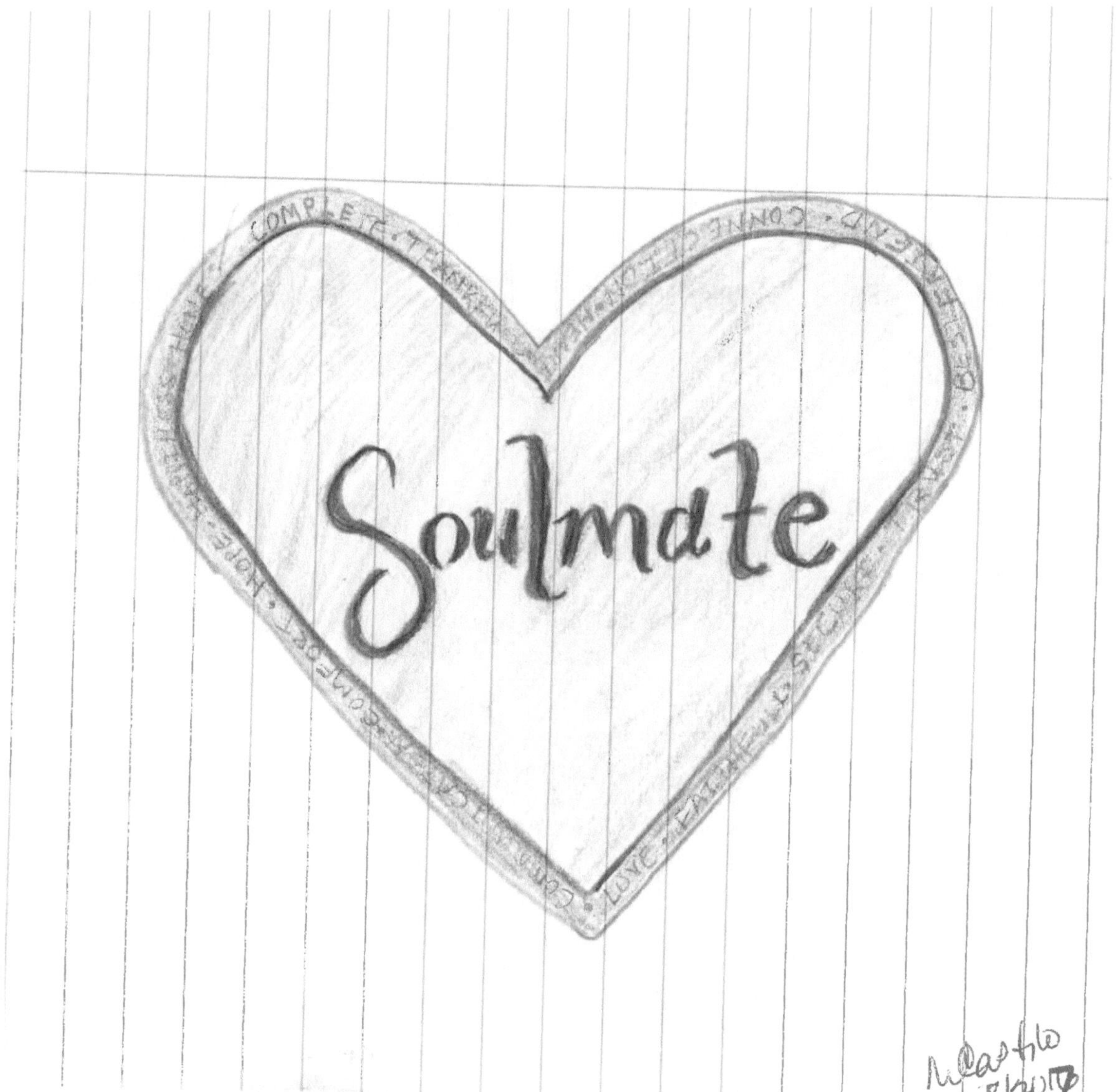
COMPLETE
CONNECTION
TRUST
Soulmate
LOVE
COMFORT
HOPE

VII. *Fear & Paranoia*

A) Questioning your own sanity. There are lots of different opinions in the world regarding spirituality and intuition- and its existence. Remain looking forward into your future and follow what universe presents to you.

B) You may come across a fear of possibly being criticized by family, friends, and/ or acquaintances. Always keep in mind- not every soul evolves at the same pace or time.

C) Learn to build boundaries to protect yourself and remain headstrong. Always engage in what will best suit yourself and will nourish your soul.

VIII. *Questioning your influence of peers*

A) Begin to breakdown who in your life will bring nourishment to your soul. More than likely it will happen on its own. Universe will step in to guide you.

B) Distance yourself from negative influence. (Debbie downers) Provide them with a link of guidance, so they may go on in their journey and find peace within themselves.

C) Start to recognize toxic weight for your soul. Toxic weight is defined as something or someone who will draw negativity to your journey.

D) Surround yourself in an environment that contributes joy, love and or complete state of bliss within your soul. Build yourself up to stand alone, proud, and dependent upon nobody.

IX. *Consider possible lifestyle changes*

A) Start to recognize who will lift your spirit and soul growth.
B) You may feel drawn to consider a change in your career. Or you could possibly come to senses of why you choose the career you are in. You will start to consider options on how to apply yourself to the world in different spiritual aspects.
C) A change in your diet may come to your mind, maybe your appetite will change. Healthy eating is a benefit to your physical body, mind, and spirit.

X. Recognize past

A) As your soul awakens, you will emerge with healthier thoughts. You will start to reflect on your past. Identify issues you could have avoided; how you could have approached situations in a healthier manner.

B) Cut any negative experimenting or habits that will not serve and benefit your body, mind & spirit. Recognize how you have been neglecting your physical body.

C) Retrain your mind, planting a positive thought train. Implement self-love, start to focus on your best qualities and embrace them.

D) Make a daily commitment to wiser and healthy ways of living. Eventually, days add up to a month and months turn into years.

E) You will come to realize that there are no mistakes on your journey. They will become lessons to gain different aspects of wisdom, to help your soul evolve.

XI. *Recognize Intuitive Abilities*

A) As your soul evolves you will become familiar with different intuitive abilities. Certain abilities will stand out to you. You will automatically know your capabilities, or the universe will guide you into further development.
B) All intuitive abilities are like muscles; we can build them up. There are exercises that can assist in building them.
C) Train yourself to become observant of your dreams. Dreams play a significant role in our spiritual practice. Start a dream journal and learn how to interpret them. They can guide you on your journey.
D) Our thoughts and intentions have energy behind them. We need to send positive thoughts and intentions into the universe. That process will help align us with positive outcomes on our journey.

Clair Abilities

I have all these abilities that I listed below.

A) **Claircognizance**- Inner knowing; Intuitive inspired wisdom.
B) **Clairaudience**- Picks up a thought and hears it like it was next to them; Telepathic
C) **Clairsentient**- Clear feeling; Catches a thought and transforms it to feelings.
D) **Claivoyance**- Ability to see things that are not present; See images in third eye.

Psychic empath

There are different types of empaths: Emotional, physical, and intuitive.
Ability to feel emotions and thoughts of another human being.
Feeling overwhelmed by these emotions. This can lead to extreme anxiety.
Feeling extreme empathy towards others.
They can pick up on non-visual, non-verbal actions when someone is feeling bliss, fear, or pain.

Telepathy

The supposed communication of thoughts or ideas by means other than the known senses.

XII. *Connect with Spirit*

Have you had loved ones pass away in life? Do you wonder if there is a after life?

    I believe there is an afterlife. I believe we are all souls in a human body. We all come to Earth to evolve. Our loved ones watch over us and can give us small signs to deliver messages and/or just let us know they are still with us. At the beginning of my spiritual awakening, I started having very intense dreams. I started to dream of people who had passed away in the tri-community I lived in. I believe I was chosen by the spirits to make their appearance and deliver a message to their loved ones. Do not ask me why I was chosen, I have no idea. I do believe everything happens for a reason. I do believe I had this spiritual awakening for a reason- Many reasons. I do take this seriously and I have no means of fibs in any way. I believe I have been chosen to connect with spirit through my dreams. I also believe anybody has the ability and can do so. I also feel there is more to my spiritual awakening behind what I can visibly see. The day will come when everything is put together. It will make better sense to me and everyone around me. I will list the ways I believe and that has been proven for me. To connect with my spirit loved ones who have passed away.

- A photo of your loved one who has passed away; Obtain an item that was theirs or an item that they gave you. Something that shared their energetic field.
- A white candle- hold the candle in your hand and set an intention (Say it out loud or in your head) You must call on that spirit to energetically reach them.
- Set up an alter like setting. While you are doing this say a prayer or say something you believe in that will call spirit and create a positive space to welcome spirit in.
- Light the candle and ask for your spirit loved ones for a sign. It can be something specific or a sign in general.
- Give spirit time to respond. It may not be the exact sign you asked for but just look out for things.
- It can be something small, something only you two know. Perhaps even a triggered memory.
- Spirits are pure energy. They deliver signs all around us every day. Maybe a feather, bird, an animal. Remember we are all connected.
- Spirit also delivers signs through electricity. I know I have personally had lights randomly blink off and on. It was always at a specific moment or time when I knew I needed a reminder that spirit was with me. I was either thinking of them or I just instantly knew in my heart it was a sign from spirit. Trust me you will know it when it happens.
- Most importantly stay open to receive information. It could be in your dreams, anything you feel can be related – Is related to spirit. Spirit wants to get messages across, they will help you. They helped me in my time of desperate need on my journey. I want people to know this exists. It can bring a person so much peace in life.

XIII. *Processing Overload*

A) You may feel an increased amount of mental pressure. Prioritize your knowledge to apply in your future.
B) Determine what is beneficial and will promote soul nourishing. Keep in mind you may come across information that you feel has no purpose of utilizing. Just remember that it may be beneficial to you in the future.
C) Be sure to take time out of each day for self-reflection.
D) Identify your own spiritual progress, you will be amazed how far you have come.

XIV. *7 Energy Chakra Centers*

Chakra- Center of spiritual power within the human body.
A) The 7 energy chakra centers are located throughout your body. This is where your physical body and your etheric body meet.
B) It is crucial that you learn and utilize your energy chakra systems. They each play a significant role to help keep us balanced.
C) Keeping energy flow and balance can help us maintain a healthy living.

1) **Root Chakra**- Located at the base of your spine. Associated with the color red. When open and in balance the root chakra helps support security, comfort, and open grounding to earth. When closed and in imbalance it can bring greed, materialistic and can resist change.
2) **Sacral Chakra**- Located at the abdomen. Associated with orange. When open and in balance the sacral chakra can support relationships, intimacy, sensuality, and emotional needs. When closed and in imbalance it can support emotionally attachment and overly sexual.
3) **Solar Plexus Chakra**- Located above your belly button. Associated with yellow. When open and in balance it can support personal power, spiritual growth, and self-confidence. When closed and in imbalance it can support the inability to set and maintain boundaries, codependency and/or addiction.
4) **Heart Chakra**- Located at heart. Associated with green. When open and in balance the heart chakra can support unconditional love, compassion, and self-love. When closed and in imbalance it can support selfishly motives, lacking motivation and /or feeling hopeless.
5) **Throat Chakra**- Located at the throat. Associated with blue. When open and in balance the throat chakra can support self-expression, communication, and independence. When closed and in imbalance it can support keeping words to a minimum and can increase shyness.
6) **Brow Chakra**- Located between your eyes- brow line. Associated with the color indigo. When open and in balance the brow chakra can support inner guidance, intuition, and our subconscious. When closed and in imbalance it can support not thinking for yourself and underactive thoughts.
7) **Crown Chakra**- Located at the top of your head. Associated with the color white and purple. When open and in balance it is in connection with your inner wisdom, meditation, and mental actions. When closed and in imbalance you may be inflexible with your own thinking and blocked by ego attachment

7 Chakras

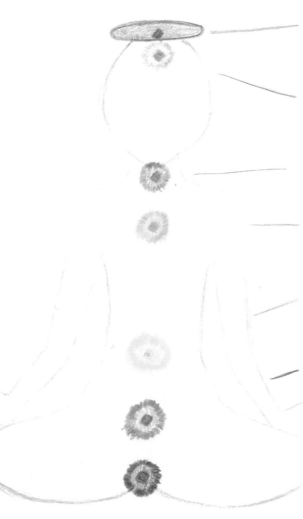

CROWN CHAKRA
INNER WISDOM, KARMA, BLISS
MEDITATION MENTAL ACTION
OVER ACTIVE - RELY ON SPIRITUALITY
BLOCKED BY - EGO ATTACHMENT

THIRD EYE CHAKRA
BALANCE HIGHER - LOWER SELF
VISUALIZATION, INTUITION
BLOCKED BY - ILLUSION

THROAT CHAKRA
Self expression, Communication
Independance, UNDER ACTIVE - SHY
THE TRUTH
BLOCKED BY - LIES

HEART CHAKRA
COMPLEX EMOTION, SELF LOVE,
COMPASSION, ACTIVE HARMONIOUS
JOY, INNER PEACE
BLOCKED BY - GRIEF

SOLAR PLEXUS CHAKRA
PERSONAL POWER, SPIRITUAL GROWTH
, SELF CONFIDENT - CONTROL LIVES
SELF WORTH, SELF ESTEEM
BLOCKED BY - SHAME

SACRAL CHAKRA ABDOMEN
RELATIONSHIP SENSUALITY
OVERLY SEXUAL, WELL BEING
SENSE OF ABUNDANCE, PLEASURE
BLOCKED BY - GUILT

ROOT CHAKRA - BASE OF SPINE
COMFORT STABILITY SECURITY
SURVIVAL , GROUND TO EARTH
RESIST CHANGE
BLOCKED BY - FEAR

CHAKRA - each of the
centers of spiritual
power in the human
body.

XV. *Raise Your Vibration*

A) Maintaining a healthy spiritual practice needs to be a daily routine; it requires work every day.
B) It is important to stay grounded. Come in actual contact with mother earth on a regular basis. Walk in your yard bare footed- touch dirt, soil and/or grass.
C) Engage in activities to enhance your life.
D) Bring out the creativity within your soul.
E) Here are some suggestions to apply to your daily routine. These are some of my favorites, but you can seek and adopt your own.

- Meditation- raise your vibration
- Daily prayer- Higher power of your choice
- Art of any type- Draw/paint (I became an artist)
- Listen to music, sing & dance (I discovered I can sing)
- Gardening-yard work or create your own garden
- Spend time in nature
- Take a bubble bath-light a candle, incorporate lavender -its known to help relax a person
- Write- Keep a daily, weekly journal. Set goals in detail-set intentions. (I wrote a book & got my associates degree)
- Always MAINTAIN a positive train of thought
- Live, Laugh & Love

XVI. *Self-acceptance*

A) Part of self-acceptance is reflecting on your past. Acknowledging your growth will help boost your self-confidence.
B) Acknowledging how you turned negative traits from your past into positive soul growth steppingstones.
C) Establish daily, monthly goal markers for yourself. To keep yourself motivated into the future.
D) Reward yourself, you have come a long way. Most importantly you deserve every ounce of it.
E) Always remember that you will keep learning within spirituality. You will come into alignment with certain soul's that will help your soul evolve on your journey.
F) There is always something new I have learned or that I am able to apply somewhere within my practice.

XVII. *Soul's Purpose*

As I emerge and blossom out of my personal spiritual awakening- My Soul's Rebirth. I believe my journey's purpose is to take on the role as a Spiritual Light Worker.

I feel my specific role is to promote unity among all nations. Promote prayer, peace, harmony, and raise spiritual awareness among the universe.

Most importantly, to remind every soul of their duty to respect & honor Universe. Timing is crucial, and we must join to aid Universe into peaceful orbiting- to the best of our ability.

Our future is dependent upon our actions- positive or negative. It is up to you all to decide. Make your actions count. Take positive action into the future for yourself, your children, and grandchildren.

1) Every soul has its own purpose in the universe. Some may be chosen to become a lightworker, others may be guided to do good within their soul in different aspects.
2) Your soul will guide you to where you are intended to be on your journey.

XVIII. *12 Universal Laws*

1) **Law of Divine Oneness**- All things are connected through creation, all life energy come from one source. Everything we do creates a ripples effect and effects the collective,

2) **Law of Vibration**- Each thought and sound have a vibrational effect. Focus on positive vibrations. Match frequencies with positive vibrations to draw into your desires and life. Everything vibrates at one speed or another.

3) **Law of Action**- Identify and align all other laws with actions. Actions will align and will bring about actions of change. This law must be exercised for us to manifest on universe.

4) **Law of Correspondence**- This law is one of the most important laws. Identify and reflect on inner reality, reflect on inner believes. Always believe that good things will come into your life.

5) **Law of Cause and Effect**- What comes around goes around. What you think and feel, will reflect to you. Focus on happiness and what you want. Every effect within our journey, upon earth has cause and an authentic staring point.

6) **Law of Compensation**- Apply cause and effect. You receive back what we send out. Universe brings back alike compensation. Any form of energy you send out, it will mirror back to you so you can manipulate it. Whether its love, envy, friendship, jealousy, hate; It all applies.

7) **Law of Attraction**- Thoughts, and actions will attract the same energy in return. What you put out; you will receive back. Influence positive vibration and you will vibrate at higher positive frequency. That vibration will be returned, and you will attract people vibrating on the same frequency. It will result in the same in a negative vibration.

8) **<u>Law of Perpetual Transmutation of Energy</u>**- Energy is in constant movement. A positive energy thought can be canceled with a negative energy thought. Universe works in our favor. It's up to us to recognize & utilize signs.

9) **<u>Law of Relativity</u>**- When presented with a challenge it is recognized as a trial. Trials are considered training for the soul; They can be embraced as a steppingstone. Send out positive vibrations of growth and confidence. Trust in Universe to align you with your path of synchronicities. This can and will shift your situation. Remain headstrong in confidence with your energies. Most of all believe in it and your world will align in success.

10) **<u>Law of Polarity</u>**- Law of opposites; Everything has an opposite. If it showed up in your life you attracted it with your thoughts, words, actions, or deeds.

11) **<u>Law of Rhythm</u>**- Energy vibrates and moves according to its own rhythm. These rhythms establish cycles and patterns. Raise your vibration and Universe will practice all other universal laws and harmonize with higher energies.

12) **<u>Law of Gender</u>**- Yin- Male positive charge/Yang- Female negative charge. All things have a period of growth before reaching its full potential of maturity. Our goal is to master the balance of masculine and feminine energies within us.

XIX. *Reach Out*

My spiritual awakening has connected me to soul callings inherited by past lives. I am currently undergoing unity with my cultures and soul relations. That will result in soul nourishment. This alone is unremarkable. It is living proof of spirituality and its existence.

These are connections that my soul has been longing for. Through-out the years of my journey, I grew inner attachments to cultures. I now have proof and reasoning why.

In my future, I have full intentions of pursuing a healthy connection with my relatives. A relationship with my relatives as we unite. Build a brighter future for universe, families, and those in need.

I have conquered many battles to get where I am today. My soul is longing for healing. Soon I will receive what is owed to me, complete soul nourishment from within.

My role as a Spiritual Light Worker will help bring peace to my soul. In addition, I will reach out to the world and assist those in need of guidance.

I will share my journey and my spiritual teaching to assist other souls on their journey. My goal is to improve people's lives, raise the growth of positive unity within humanity. Act upon healing of which I am capable.

The universe will guide and introduce new leaders in the future. True leaders join, learn from each other, and unite. Implementing beneficial changes and brainstorming together for the better of the universe.

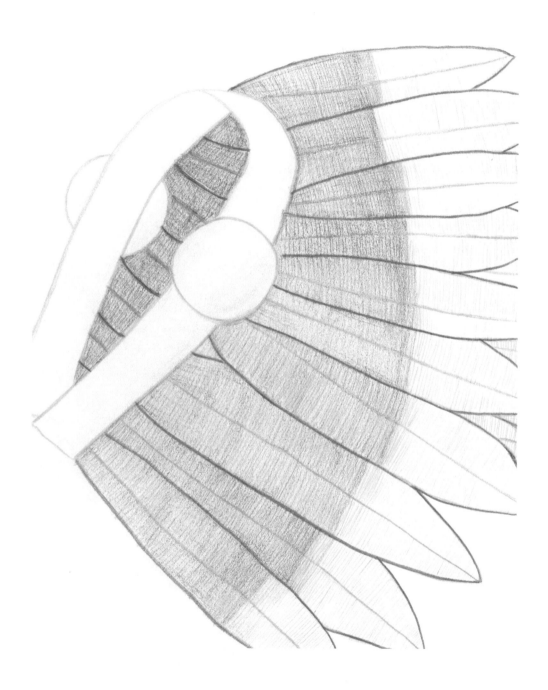

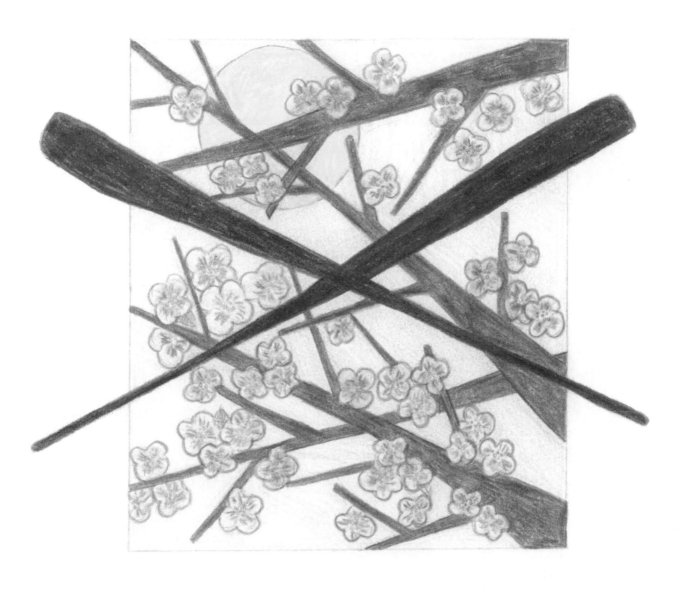

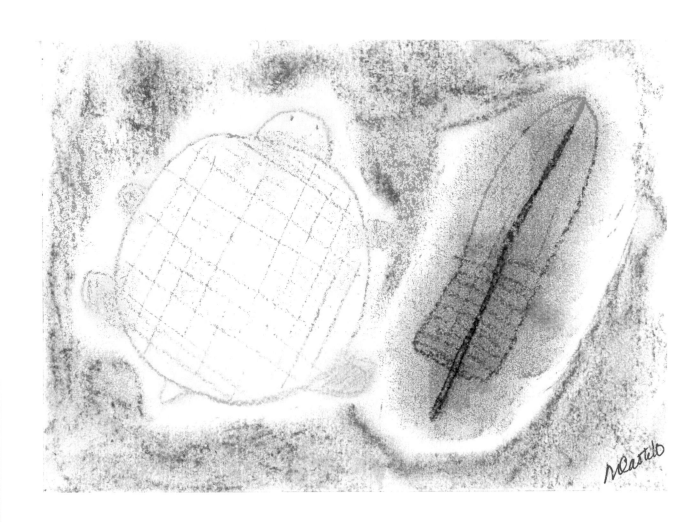

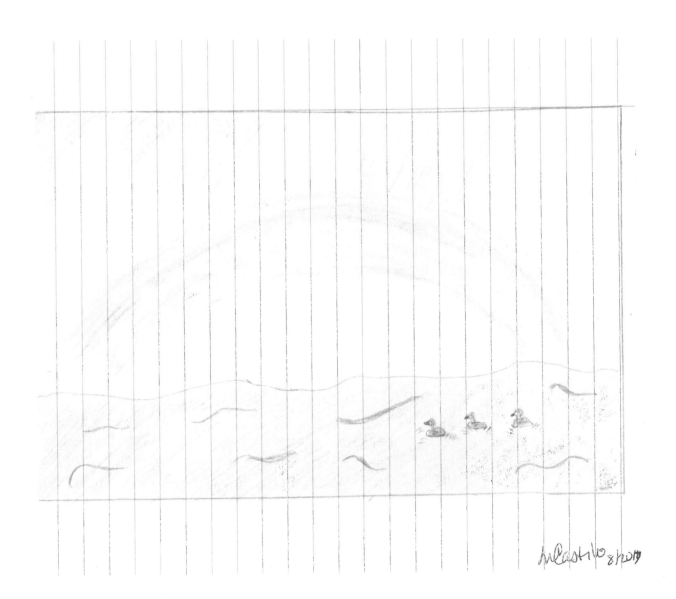

XX. *Conclusion*

After reading this book I hope I made my point of what it took for me to stumble across my intuition. I hope you were able to identify how far I was pushed mentally to get me where I am today. I went through a lot for me to awaken to my intuition ability. This may not be the case for everybody. I also pointed out the different definitions of intuition. Gave specific ways to higher your vibration, connect with spirit and how to recognize and utilize the 7 chakras.

This book is just an outline of how things came to me in my up close and personal spiritual awakening. Everybody will have their own, at their own pace and different abilities. I feel so inclined to share mine with the world. I want to make it clear that I do not have all the answers. My answers and ways may not be the exact same way as yours or anyone else's. But I did get results in my spiritual awakening. I am alive and living proof of my spirit awakening. Last words to you all would be: Follow your intuition, it is there and tugging at you for a reason.

Thank you for purchasing my book and taking my words into your journey.

Printed in the United States
by Baker & Taylor Publisher Services